DAVID PAUL WERNER

CHAK MAN ANDREW YIP

TEN BAGATELLES
for Organ

Four Friendly Pieces

Three Celebratory Toccatas

Christian Arts Foundation

CAF

Christian Arts Foundation
www.caf.org.hk

Performance notes

Registrations suggested here are for a quintessential 2-manual chapel or school organ (exemplified below). They serve as liberal guides to timbre, balance and overarching effect.

"Chant donné" and *"Jig for Reeds"* were composed for one manual. More elaborate registrations here take advantage of two manuals and optional pedal.

The following conventions are used in notation:

· Common notes passing from one voice to another are often not shown as tied, but in legato playing are to be tied unless [1] a rearticulation (/) is explicitly indicated, or [2] it would result in a tie to a descending melodic line on the same manual.

· Dynamics from *pp* to *f* indicate relative position of expression shutters, from fully closed to fully open.

· Wedges ($<$ $>$) or text *cresc.* and *dim.* indicate gradual opening and closing of expression shutters.

· +Reg. and −Reg. means to add and remove registers (*i.e.*, stops), respectively.

· *ff* indicates full or relatively full organ with expression shutters open.

· Divisional abbreviations are G or Gt. for Great (primary manual), S or Sw. for Swell (subordinate manual), and Ped. for Pedal.

· GS on manual staves means play on Great with Swell coupled.

· G, S or GS on the pedal staff indicates which manuals are to be coupled to the pedal.

· Solo on the pedal staff means no manual-to-pedal couplers are engaged.

D. P. W.

Zhejiang Conservatory of Music, Hangzhou, China
Freiburger, 2018

Grand Orgue	Récit expressif	Pédale
Montre 8	Flûte traversière 8	Soubasse 16
Flûte harmonique 8	Viole de Gambe 8	Flûte 8
Bourdon 8	Voix céleste 8	Bourdon 8
Prestant 4	Flûte octaviante 4	Basson 16
Flûte à cheminée 4	Nazard 2²/₃	
Doublette 2	Octavin 2	
Fourniture IV	Hautbois 8	
Trompette 8	Trémolo	
	Subkoppel	

Estación de Kobe wedding hall, Kobe, Japan
Mana (マ ナ), 1996

Hauptwerk	Schwellwerk	Pedal
Prinzipal 16	Bourdon 8	Principal 16
Prestant 8	Salicional 8	Bourdon 16
Flute 8	Traverso 4	Octave 8
Octave 4	Waldfloete 2	Octave 4
Superoctave 2	Sesquialter II	Fagott 16
Mixture III-IV	Clarinet 8	Trumpet 8
Spanish Trumpet 8	Tremulant	

FOUR FRIENDLY PIECES

Chant donné

David Paul Werner

Gt.: Flute 8'
Sw.: Bourdon 8', Vox Humana, Trem.
(try String 8', Flute 4' in lieu of Vox Humana)
Ped.: Soft 16' or 8', Sw. or Gt. to Ped.

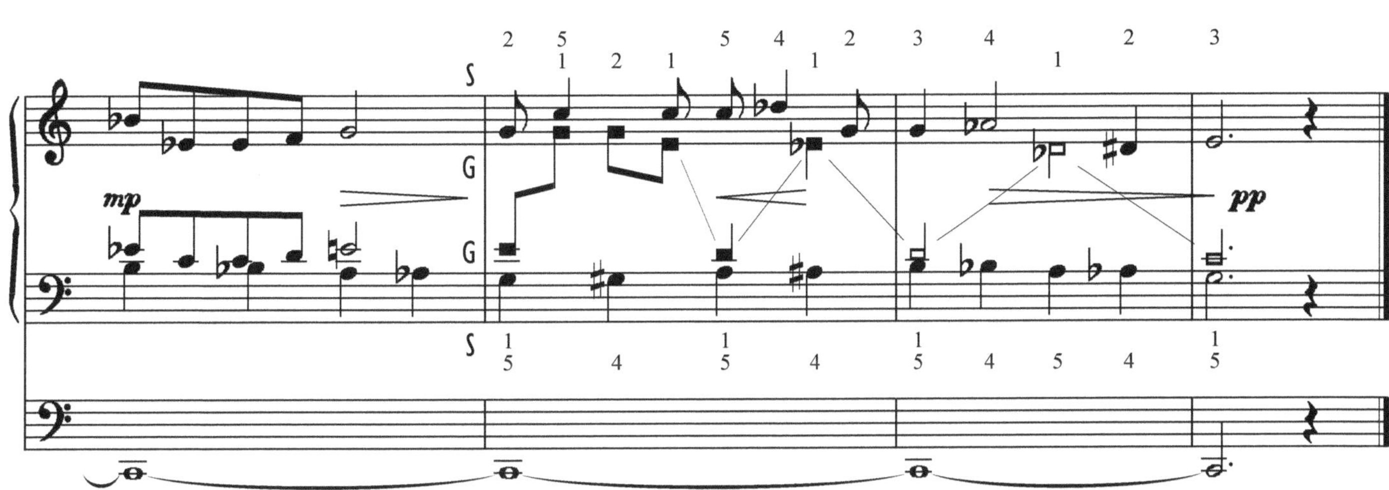

Jig for Reeds

Man.: Reeds dominant

chiara   a tempo
(no rit.)
D.S. %
1st reg. f
CODA
tempo giusto fino alla fine
3
2
ff

Elegy

Flowers drifted down over the light
coming from her: roses and daffodils
and poppies and bluebells floated on by.

mf
S p
Ped. S
Ped. GS
+ Sw. Fl. 8'
+ Sw. Fl. 4'
f mp
+ Sw. Diapason, Oboe
+ Gt. Diapason 8'
cresc. poco a poco
GS
GS
sub.
p
GS
più lento
S
quasi a tempo
ritard.
opt. 8va
f
S
opt. 8vb
p
Sw. 1st reg.
Ped. S
Ped. 1st reg. solo
If a balanced sub-harmonic effect of two pedal notes is not
possible, omit the upper pedal notes these last three bars.

Rumba real

Come una danza maestosa ♩=60

GS

Gt.: Foundations 16' 8' 4'
Sw.: Full 8' 4' 2'
Ped.: Foundations 16' 8'

S
2/4
4/4
p
GS
Reduce Gt. (16' off)
4/4
GS
mp

ff (+16')
Ped. GS

Più largo
Riten.
8va
Alt. ending for manuals to a''':
Più largo
Riten.

THREE CELEBRATORY TOCCATAS
Toccata Concertino

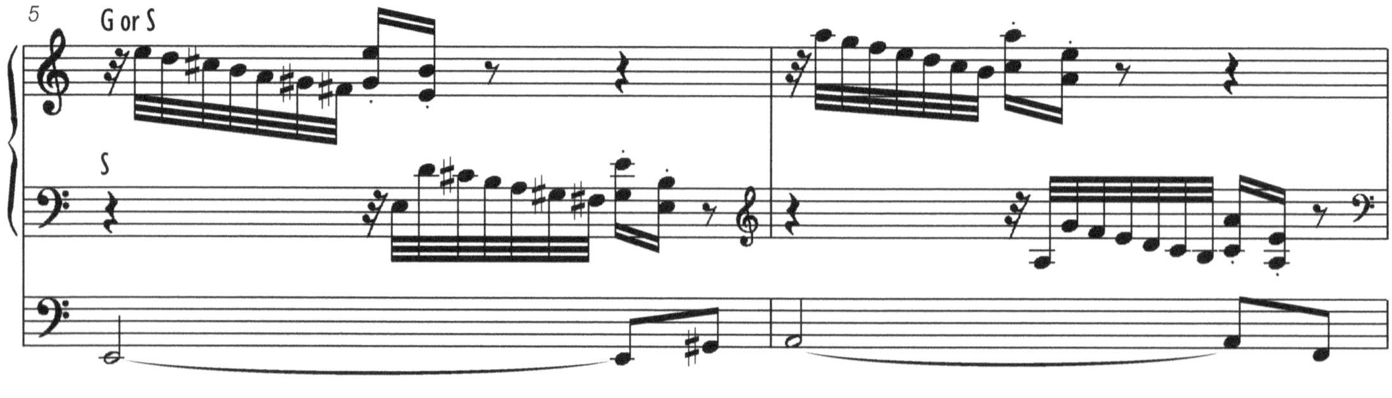

This opening and closing section is most naturally playable on three
manuals. Annotations here use Swell expression to emulate three.
For two manuals unexpressed, simply change manuals as indicated.

15
Gt. Mild 8' (Trem.)
Adagietto espressivo
Sw. String 8'
GS espressione a piacere
S
Ped.
smorz.
Man.
20
riten.
f mp
24
a tempo
28
teneramente
ritard.
Ped.
32
a tempo
G +8' (−Trem.)
S +Flutes 8' 4', Trompette or Oboe
36
un poco più animato
GS
p
cresc. poco a poco
+Reg.
f
+Gt. Prin. 4' 2'

ritard.
40
sostenuto
Ped. GS + Foundations 16' 8'
Adagietto
Andante risoluto
44
S { String 8'
G {
1st reg. —16'
Soft 16'
Ped. S, 1st reg.
49
riten.
52
D.S.
+16'
Ped. GS

Toccata Sognai

manuals-only version
(original version overleaf)

Man.: Full and bright, with 16'

Toccata Sognai

26
tr
3
S
GS
S
legato
31
ritard.
a tempo
37
GS
meno legato
allargando
41
ff
(Opt. l.h. on Solo reeds)

Toccata Breve

rall. poco a poco
cresc.
f
a tempo
ff
14
riten.
a tempo
riten.

Presage & Anachronous Fugue

David Paul Werner

Presage

Nunc lento sonitu dicunt, morieris.

Gt.: Soft Foundations 16' 8' 4'
     (no Gt. Mixtures throughout)
Sw.: Full
Ped.: Bourdons 16' 8'

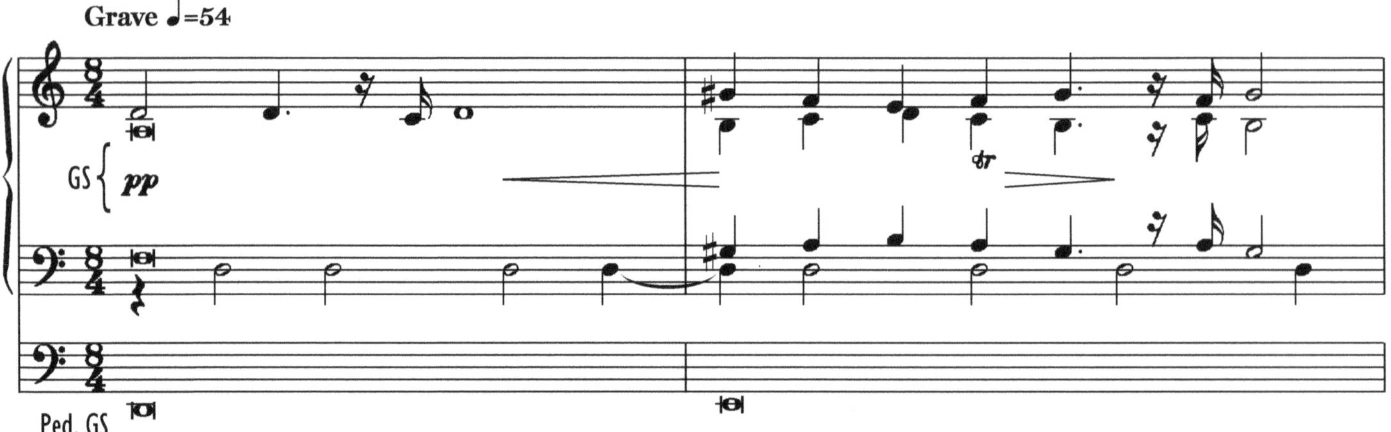

un poco agitato
largando
+Octave
crescendo poco a poco
Tempo I°
f +12th, 15th
+Ped. Diapasons 16' 8'
ff +Reeds 16' 8'
+Ped. 32' or 10-2/3'
+Ped. Reeds

Anachronous Fugue

La Mort t'admire en tes contorsions, risible Humanité.

Gt.: Foundations 8'
Sw.: Foundations 8' 4' 2', Mix.
Ped.: Foundations 16' 8'

GS
Ped. S

S { +Sw. Reed
+Gt. Octave 4'
un pochino meno mosso
GS
rall. gradualmente

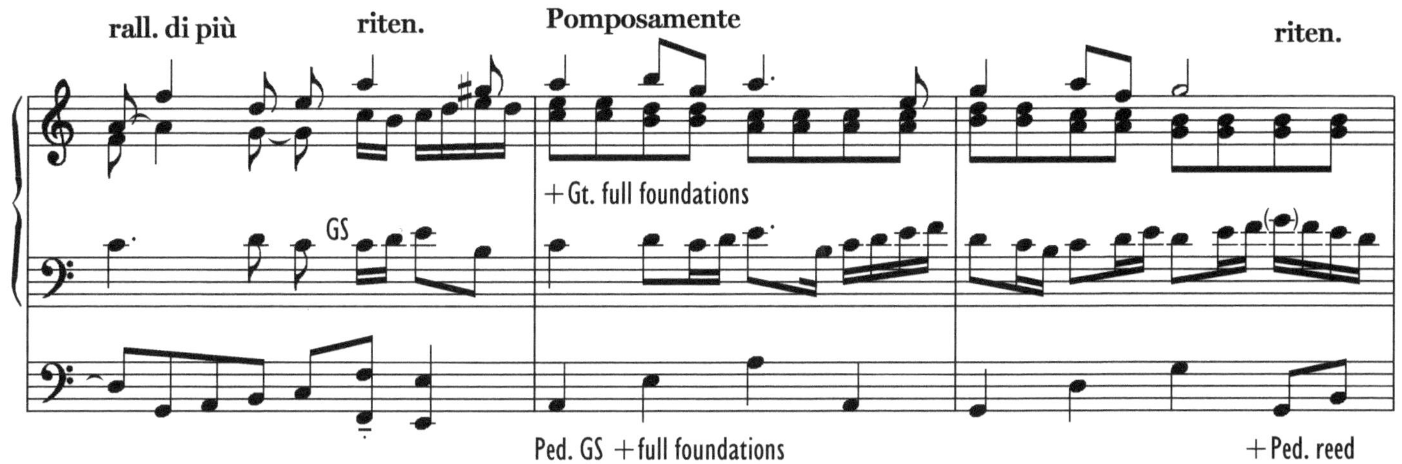

rall. di più
riten.
Pomposamente
riten.
+Gt. full foundations
GS
Ped. GS +full foundations
+Ped. reed

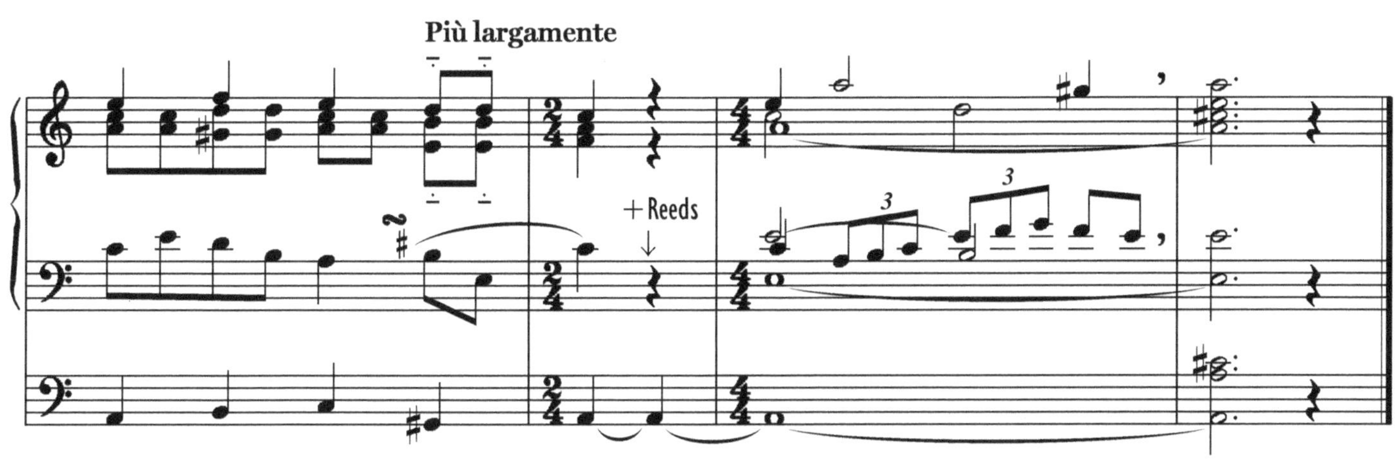

Più largamente
+Reeds
3
3

Alternate endng
3

LOOKS LIKE RAIN

Chak Man Andrew Yip

Three well-balanced voices, distinct but without
sharp contrast, as would be true of a string trio.

rall.   esitare   a tempo
rall.   meno mosso

ARRIVAL OF THE QUEEN OF SHEBA

G. F. Handel, HWV 67
arr. D. P. Werner

36
G
G
39
S
42
G
45
S
48
G
51

72
75
78
G
GS
(Ped.)
81
84
87

www.ingramcontent.com/pod-product-compliance
Lightning Source LLC
Chambersburg PA
CBHW040157110726
48005CB00018B/2791